D1473595

Made in United States
Orlando, FL
01 March 2022

15283208R00067